CATERPILLAR TRAIL

Based on the BBC television series,
Caterpillar Trail encourages young children
to have fun by becoming physically involved
in exploring the natural life around them –
from making a fishing net out of a
coat-hanger and discovering tadpoles, to
smelling grass and hugging trees!

Come along! Just follow the trail.

Penny Lloyd works in the BBC TV's
Children's Department as a
director of 'Playschool' as well as
producer of 'Caterpillar Trail'.

THE COUNTRY CODE

Read it . . . obey it . . . then you will always be welcome and happy in our countryside.

1 Guard against all risks of fire.
2 Fasten all gates.
3 Keep dogs under proper control.
4 Keep to the paths across farmland.
5 Avoid damaging fences, hedges and walls.
6 Leave no litter.
7 Safeguard water supplies.
8 Protect wildlife, wild plants and trees.
9 Go carefully on country roads.
10 Respect the life of the countryside.

Rules 8 and 10 include taking *greatest possible care* of small animals which you have collected. Keep them in suitable containers, under good conditions. Treat them gently. Try to find out which food they normally eat and give them a supply of this. Some animals do not feed in captivity. These animals should be returned to the wild the same day.

 If you are ever unsure about following the ideas suggested on the trail, always ask the person who looks after you if he or she will come along too to help you.

CATERPILLAR TRAIL

PENNY LLOYD

Illustrated by Joanna Cheese

BBC/KNIGHT BOOKS

Text copyright © Penny Lloyd 1987
Illustrations copyright © British Broadcasting Corporation 1987

First published by Knight Books 1987

British Library C.I.P.

Lloyd, Penny
  Caterpillar trail.
  1. Biology – Juvenile literature
  I. Title   II. Cheese, Joanna
  III. British Broadcasting Corporation
  574   QH092

  ISBN 0-340-40603-8
    (0-563-20536-9) BBC

Printed and bound in Great Britain for the British
Broadcasting Corporation, 35 Marylebone High Street,
London W1M 4AA and Hodder and Stoughton
Paperbacks, a division of Hodder and Stoughton Ltd.,
Mill Road, Dunton Green, Sevenoaks, Kent (Editorial
Office: 47 Bedford Square, London WC1B 3DP) by
Cox & Wyman Ltd., Reading, Berks.
Photoset by Rowland Phototypesetting Ltd.,
Bury St Edmunds, Suffolk.

CONTENTS

FOREWORD

As long as I can remember, I have been interested in nature. I was forever bringing 'interesting things' home to my long suffering mother . . . like bones, snails' shells, owl pellets, etc! It doesn't matter whether you live in the countryside or in the middle of a big city, wherever you live you are surrounded by nature. You just have to look under a stone, go for a walk in the park, or even sit at your window!

As you read through this book, you will find some sections that we have touched on in the television series, and others we haven't got round to yet. Each section includes suggestions of things that you can do to help you spot and jot, and the ideas cover all of the seasons. Remember that this book is a guide and if you become really interested in any section of it, you can carry on and create your own project. If you like, you could write to me at *Caterpillar Trail* and let me know what you are doing.

If you are not already a member of a nature club and would like to join one, you will find some useful addresses at the end of this book. Joining a club is a very good idea; you'll make new friends and meet people with similar interests, and of course learn new things all the time.

I hope you'll have lots of fun reading this book and answering the questions it sets out for you. Don't forget to let me know how you get on.

Keep spotting and jotting.
Good luck.

Stuart Bradley

Mini beasts!

Insects and small animals in your house, park or garden.

Can you spot ....

an ant?

An ant doesn't have a back bone. How many parts is its body divided into? ....

What else can you spot with the same number of legs? Count its legs. How many? ....

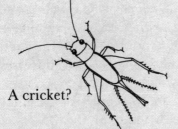

A cricket uses its back legs to sing with – it rubs them together.

A cricket?

A fly?

A fly tastes with its feet.

A bee?

A bee uses *two* pairs of wings to fly. They are joined together by special hooks.

1

All spiders have ....

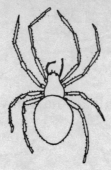

Eight legs!

Spiders can be very useful around the house. They eat lots of flies and other pests.

A spider spins a silken web to catch its prey, but it doesn't stick itself because it has oil on its feet.

Have you ever spotted anything caught in a web?

What? ....

A money spider is very small. If you spot one crawling on you it is supposed to bring you luck.

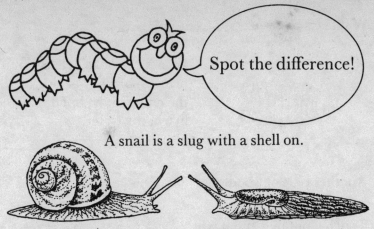

Spot the difference!

A snail is a slug with a shell on.

Slugs and snails have no feet. They make a slimy substance which helps them to move along on their belly. It also helps us to spot them! Why not follow a shiny track on the pavement, and see where it leads to ....

When the weather is very dry or cold, the snail pulls its body inside its shell, and seals itself in until the weather improves.

See if you can find any treasure in your garden. You might find an empty snail shell, that a bird has left behind after a tasty meal.

Slugs and snails like to live in damp places, under plants or stones, or in the soil.

3

What else can you spot?

Woodlice like to live in damp places too. They belong to the crab family, but don't live in the water.

Another type of woodlouse . . . a pill bug.

Touch a pill bug and it will roll into a ball to protect itself. What else does this?

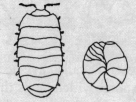

A Hedgehog

Watch a worm and see if you can spot how it moves along.

Which is the front? . . . the end with the mouth! Can you spot the mouth?

WHAT ELSE CAN YOU SPOT?

Feed the birds!

How many different birds can you spot from your window? ....
In the summer months birds find plenty of food – insects, seeds and berries – for themselves, but in the winter when food is scarce, they may need some help from you. Here are some things you could do:

Leave fresh water out for them (make sure it doesn't freeze!).

A small brown bird with a red breast and white tummy?

A Robin

Leave scraps or crusts on a bird-table or window-sill (if it is very cold you can soak the crusts in warm water).

A bird with black feathers and a yellow beak?

A Male Blackbird

5

It is best to feed birds above the ground so that cats or dogs won't attack them (or steal their food!).

Fill a plastic-mesh bag, the kind that oranges are sometimes sold in, with nuts or scraps, and hang it up outside. Then watch and see which birds come and peck through the holes. What can you spot?

Thread monkey-nuts on a string and hang them up.

Or hang up half a coconut!

A small bird with a blue cap, black collar, blue wings and yellow tummy.

A Bluetit

If you do decide to feed the birds in winter you must feed them regularly, as they will rely on you, and only stop feeding gradually, when the weather gets warmer.

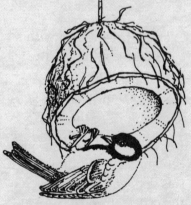

A bird with green and blue wings, a black cap and collar and a black stripe down its yellow tummy?

A Male Great Tit

Make your own bird bell

Cut the top off a plastic lemonade bottle.

Cover the bottom with a piece of plastic mesh-bag.

Hold it in place with an elastic band.

Unscrew the top and fill the bell with nuts.

Ask an adult to help.

Make a hole in the top and then thread a loop of string through it.

Put the top back on the bell and hang it from a branch or window catch.

Experiment with different scraps and see which birds like which food best. Jot down what you discover.

How many of these birds can you spot?

Swallow . . . .   Starling . . . .
Robin . . . .   Greenfinch . . . .
Wren . . . .   Great tit . . . .
Blackbird . . . .   Pigeon . . . .
Thrush . . . .   House Martin . . . .
Sparrow . . . .   Magpie . . . .
Bluetit . . . .   Lapwing . . . .

Which of them do you only see in the summer? . . . .

. . . .

. . . .

. . . .

Listening!

Find somewhere comfortable to sit outside and try listening to your own breathing.

Now close your eyes and listen to the sounds around you. What can you hear? Jot them down here . . .

How many different bird songs can you identify?

....

Do you know who is making them? Write it down . . .

Open your eyes and see if you can spot the birds.

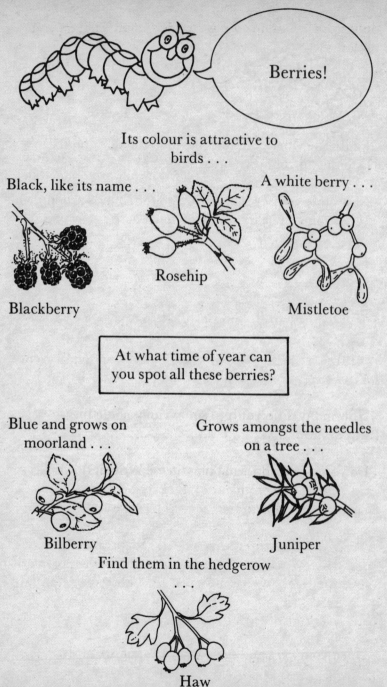

Berries!

Its colour is attractive to birds . . .

Black, like its name . . .

Blackberry

Rosehip

A white berry . . .

Mistletoe

At what time of year can you spot all these berries?

Blue and grows on moorland . . .

Bilberry

Grows amongst the needles on a tree . . .

Juniper

Find them in the hedgerow . . .

Haw

Split open a rosehip with your fingernail. What do you find inside?

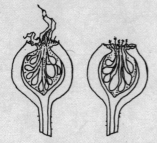

Every berry has seeds inside it, which can grow into new plants if they are planted in suitable ground.

Here are some ways that the seeds are planted:

A bird eats the berry and drops the seeds, or wipes them off its beak onto the soil.

The berry dies and falls to the ground where the seeds go into the earth.

If someone treads on a berry and squashes it, the seeds may be carried on the sole of their shoe, and then planted. (Seeds can travel quite a long way!)

A bird or creature eats a berry, the seeds travel through its body, come out in its droppings, and are then planted (sometimes far away from where the berry was eaten!)

Can you think of any other ways?

Next time you spot a berry growing, see if you can guess how it was first planted.

Can you spot berries growing on plants with leaves like these?

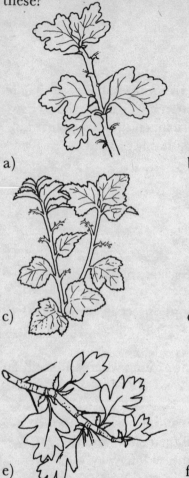

a)

b)

c)

d)

e)

f)

Draw in the berries.

Do you know what any of them are called? If not, the answers are at the bottom of the page.

e) **Hawthorn** f) **Grape**

a) **Gooseberry** b) **Holly** c) **Blackcurrant** d) **Strawberry**

Rainbow spotting!

Choose a place to sit outdoors. How many different natural colours can you spot around you?

....

Do you know what colours these should be?

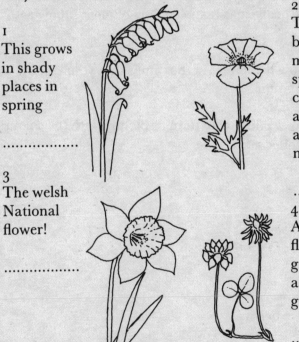

1
This grows in shady places in spring

....

2
These can be found making splashes of colour along roads and motorways

....

3
The welsh National flower!

....

4
A wild flower that grows amongst grass

....

Can you find out what their names are?
Try to copy the colour of the flower exactly, and colour the pictures in.

1. Bluebell   2. Poppy   3. Daffodil   4. Clover.

Which is your favourite colour?

....

Can you spot six natural things in your favourite colour?
What are they?

1)   4)

2)   5)

3)   6)

Without picking anything living (although you can take
tiny pieces!) collect as many colours of the rainbow as
you can.

Do you know the names of the things that your colours
have come from?

Try making a rainbow pattern or picture with the colours
you have collected:

Pond life!

Look at the plants growing on a pond. Can you spot which ones are floating and which have roots?

:Don't get too near the edge!

Hornwort flowers under the water. It floats!

The yellow water-lily has a large seedpod. When it is ripe it floats away and sinks so the seeds are planted in the pond bed.

Can you spot how duckweed grows?

This is called a water soldier, because it has leaves like swords. It usually grows under the water.

Can you guess what this is called? (The shape of the leaves gives a clue.)

An Arrowhead

15

What can you spot on the pond?

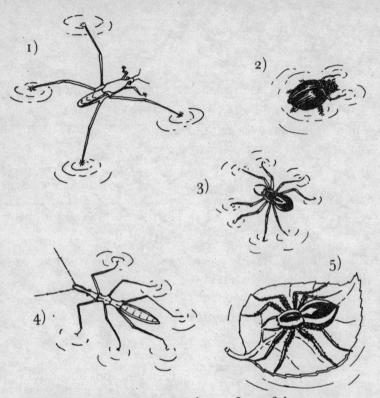

1. A *pond skater* skates across the surface of the water
   looking for insects to eat!
2. *Whirligig beetles* use their hairy legs like oars to swim in
   circles. If they spot danger they dive quickly down to
   the bottom, taking an air bubble with them.
3. This daring *pirate spider* doesn't spin a web. It hunts
   for its food by running across the water's surface, or
   diving underneath. It doesn't mind getting wet!
4. *Watermeasurers* (look like small pond skaters!) have a
   layer of hair on their bodies to keep them dry!
5. *Raft spiders* are very fierce and float on pieces of leaf or
   twigs to hunt. When they catch something they bring
   it on board to eat!

Many other strange creatures live in the murky depths.
If you would like to spot them, you will need:

A net!

An old
washing-
up bowl!

A
spoon!

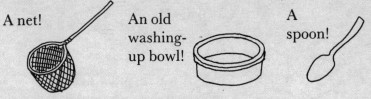

(You could make the net out
of a wire coat-hanger and a
pair of tights.)

This is what to do.

Put some pond water in the
washing-up bowl. (Be
careful not to fall in!)

Dip the net deeply into the
pond. Try not to scrape the
bottom or you will have a
net full of mud!

Lift the net out and see what you've caught!

Use a spoon to lift the
creature off the net and into
the bowl so you can have a
closer look at it.

Jot down everything you spot, then carefully empty the
creatures back into the pond.

17

Creatures of the murky depths!

Do you recognise any of these?

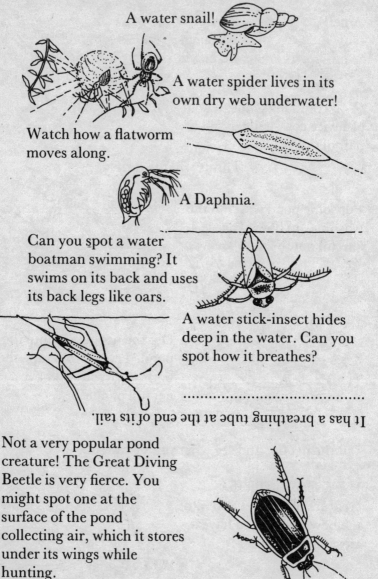

A water snail!

A water spider lives in its own dry web underwater!

Watch how a flatworm moves along.

A Daphnia.

Can you spot a water boatman swimming? It swims on its back and uses its back legs like oars.

A water stick-insect hides deep in the water. Can you spot how it breathes?

It has a breathing tube at the end of its tail.

Not a very popular pond creature! The Great Diving Beetle is very fierce. You might spot one at the surface of the pond collecting air, which it stores under its wings while hunting.

What else can you spot? ....

Tadpoles!

If you go pond dipping in the spring you might be lucky enough to collect some frogspawn. You could keep it in pond water and watch the tadpoles develop, but return the tadpoles to the pond before they are fully grown.

A frog tadpole!

Do you recognise this
tadpole?
It isn't a frog, it's a newt!

Newts spend most of their time on the land, but breed in water. The eggs are laid singly and take about three weeks to develop into a tadpole. These take a much longer time to grow than frog tadpoles and stay in the pond all summer.

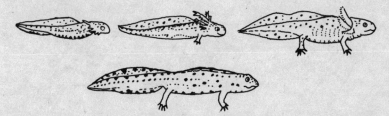

Young newts usually crawl out of the pond by the end of the summer to shelter under nearby stones.

Can you spot . . .
a frog? ....
a toad? ....
a newt? ....
or a dragonfly? ....

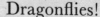

Dragonflies!

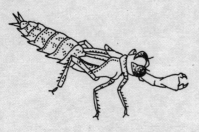

This ugly creature is a dragonfly nymph. After hatching out of its egg, laid below the water, it crawls to the bottom of the pond where it lives for several years before it is able to crawl out of the water.

When it does, this is what happens: ....

Early in the morning, it climbs to the top of a reed, and clinging on very tightly, its dull skin splits at the neck and a beautiful insect slowly begins to emerge. . . .

It pulls itself slowly out, head first . . .

releases one pair of legs at a time, and leaving behind

its ugly case, it flips itself the right way up.

Pausing for a rest while it dries out, its beautiful wings become clear and shiny.

And then, completely transformed, the dragonfly flies
away to join other dragonflies and find a mate.

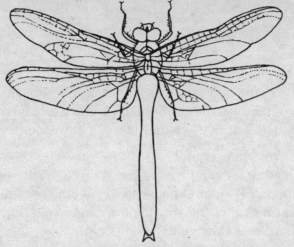

Can you spot an empty nymph case? ....
Take a note of the colour of a dragonfly and colour in
the above picture.

Watch a dragonfly flying – it can hover and even fly
backwards. Can you see how it uses its two pairs of
wings alternately?

Dragonflies have a very short life.
Jot down the first
date that you spot one this year ....

and the latest date ....

How many can you spot in one day? ....

or during the whole summer? ....

You may not see any dragonflies over the winter,
but the nymphs are hiding, and growing at the bottom
of the pond, waiting for their transformation day.

Small animals can be very shy creatures. They like
hiding, so the best places to spot them are holes, hedges,
trees and ditches. The most likely times to see them are
at dawn and dusk when they leave home to look for food.

What you will need:-
1) An adult for company.
2) Patience (you might have to wait a long time!).
3) Warm clothes (dawn and dusk can be cold times!).
4) Sharp eyes (binoculars might help!).

Some easy animals to spot:

Most squirrels live in trees.
Their nests are called dreys.
They eat nuts, fruit, cones
and seeds. Red squirrels are
quite rare, but there are
plenty of grey squirrels to be
seen. If you spot a squirrel,
keep very still and it may
come close to have a look at
you!

You are most likely to spot a
hedgehog at night. Listen
for them snuffling or
rustling leaves. Try leaving
a saucer of bread and milk
out, and then hide and see
how many hungry
hedgehogs you can spot!

22

Harvest mice are very small. They build their nests in country fields round blades of grass. By the end of the summer, when the grass has grown, they may have to jump a long way from nest to ground! If you spot a nest, keep watch by it and see if a mouse comes out!

You can tell a vole from a mouse because it has a shorter face and tail, and small ears. Field voles live in grassland, dunes and woods. In the winter they make tunnels under the snow. You may spot one gnawing at the bark of a tree.

Shrews have long, twitching, whiskery snouts! They eat beetles, slugs and worms, as well as some plants, and like to live in thick undergrowth. Water shrews live along the banks of streams and rivers. They swim very well, and if you disturb one you may hear a splash as it jumps into the water. Can you spot one swimming? What colour does it look in the water? ....

Spot a molehill. This will show you where a mole lives. They dig long tunnels with their shovel-shaped feet, and push surplus soil to the surface. Old molehills have grass growing on them, if the earth is fresh then the molehill is new. Moles spend most of their time under-ground and usually come out at night. This makes them difficult to spot. They are very partial to earthworms, and you may be lucky enough to see one looking for worms after heavy rain!

How many of these small animals can you spot?

ANIMAL	WHERE?	WHEN?
Weasel		
Rabbit		
Squirrel		
Mouse		
Hare		
Vole		
Hedgehog		

What else can you spot?

Night fliers!

There are over fifteen different types of bats in Britain. The two most common are . . .

The Pipistrelle

and

The Long-Eared Bat.

Bats hunt at night time. They catch insects while they are flying. The long-eared bat likes to rest while eating; he will often have a favourite eating perch where he hangs upside down to eat a tasty meal.

Have you ever spotted a bat? If you spot one asleep or hibernating, do not disturb it as they are very easily frightened, and might die of shock.

25

A bat's wing is said to be
very like a human hand.
Can you spot four fingers
and a thumb?

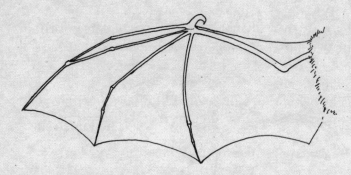

The saying 'As blind as a bat' is false – bats can see very
well! As well as sight, bats use a form of sonar (echo
navigation) to find their way around. They make high
pitched noises, which echo back to them when they are
near objects and stop them flying into things! We can't
hear these noises, but some insects can; they hear the
bats coming and escape being eaten!

Pipistrelles and long-eared bats like to roost in trees and
houses. They can squeeze themselves into very tiny
spaces –

> Between rafters
> Under tiles
> Under flat roofs
> In hollow walls.

In the winter, bats leave their roost to find a cold, dark
place to hibernate. Before hibernating they have to eat a
lot – to keep them going through the winter.

How to tell where bats are roosting.

Look for:

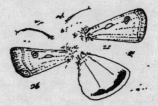

Droppings! Bat droppings look like mouse droppings, but if you rub them between finger and thumb they crumble to dust.

Left-overs from mealtimes! If you find moth or insect wings on the floor, you may be near a bat feeding-perch.

If you think you have found a roost, sit outside it at dusk. If you are right, you will see all the bats leave, one after the other, to go hunting.

If you would like bats to roost near your home, you could make or buy a bat box.

If you write to the *Fauna and Flora Preservation Society*, they will tell you how to make one. (Find their address at the end of this book.)

Smells!

Use your nose!

Try smelling:

A rose .... (What does it smell like?)
A buttercup ....
The grass ....
A tree ....
Crispy leaves ....

How do smells change in the rain, or at different times of the year?

Ask a friend to take you for a walk around the park, or the school field, while you have your eyes closed. Try and remember all the smells. Guess what they are. Do the walk again, this time with your eyes open, and see if you were right.

What did you smell?

....

....

....

....

Nesting!

From late spring through to the end of summer, is a very busy time for birds. If you spot some birds carrying things in their beaks then, they will probably be building nests or feeding their young.

Can you spot any nests?

....

Here are some of the places to look for them:-
Gaps in buildings
Drainpipes
Streetlamps
Trees
Hedges
On cliffs
Amongst the grass
Nest boxes
Barns

Remember! You must never disturb breeding birds or their nests and eggs (it's against the law). You can watch from a safe distance though, and observe the baby birds!

Some nests to spot:

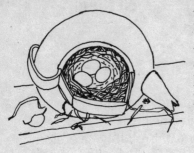

A Robin's nest is made of moss, grass and leaves. Almost any site will do – on a shelf in a shed, in a tree hole, or even in an old pot or kettle!

A Moorhen builds its nest near water. The nest is a platform made of reeds.

Buildings with eaves are the places to look for House Martin nests! They are round nests made of mud and cemented under eaves or bridges. The entrance is at the top!

Birds' eggs come in many different colours and sizes. If you spot any of these, draw and colour the egg:

ROBIN (white with red/brown spots)
MOORHEN (Beige with reddish blotches)
HOUSE MARTIN (White!)

A Nuthatch builds it nest inside a tree. It is made of bark flakes or dead leaves. A small bird, the Nuthatch plasters mud around the entrance – leaving only a tiny hole, so the nest is safe from bigger birds!

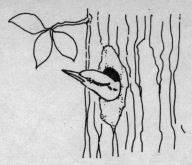

A dome-shaped nest, high in a tree or bush, may belong to a Magpie. Their nests are made of twigs and are lined with mud.

Blue Tits build nests of wool, moss, grass and hair. They like nesting in bird-boxes, but you may also find nests in tree holes, or walls.

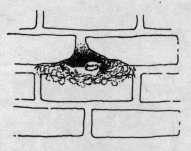

If you spot a nest near you, watch the birds and note when they leave the nest. Perhaps they fly south for the winter?

BIRD	TYPE OF NEST	WHEN THEY LEAVE

Make a nesting supermarket!

If you would like to help birds make their nests you could provide some materials.

Hang up bits of wool, straw and string from a tree

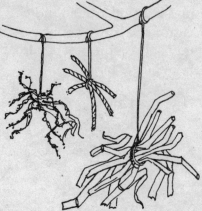

or collect old leaves, feathers, small twigs, and moss (as well as wool, etc.) and fill a mesh bag. Hang it from a tree or window and see who your customers are!

To find out what your customers want, keep a note of what different birds use which nesting materials.

	WOOL	STRING	STRAW	FEATHER
ROBIN				
TIT				
SPARROW				
PIGEON				
MAGPIE				
MARTIN				

Cuckoo!

The cuckoo fosters its babies out to other birds!

Each mother cuckoo scouts around looking for foster parents. She watches other birds building their nests.

She waits until the mother bird leaves the nest, then removes an egg and leaves one of her own in its place!

Cuckoos often lay their eggs in the nest of the type of bird that was their own foster parent. They can even lay an egg the same colour as the other ones in the nest so the foster parent may not even notice!

One female cuckoo can lay up to thirteen eggs, each in a different nest!

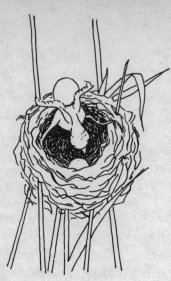

Because it is so greedy the baby cuckoo throws the other eggs out of the nest. It has a hollow in its back into which it fits the eggs and then tips them over the side!

The young cuckoo can quickly outgrow its foster parents, who work very hard to feed it. Often it cries so much that other parent birds flying past take pity on it and feed it the food meant for their own hungry babies!

Three weeks after hatching the young cuckoo leaves the nest. Two weeks later it is completely independent.

Listen for a cuckoo in spring time.

What date do you first hear it? ....

How many times can you hear a cuckoo call in one day?

A feely trail!

Have you ever felt a holly leaf or a rose petal?
Choose a place outside and test the texture of the things
around you. See what you can find that is ....

soft ....

prickly ....

tickly ....

hairy ....

damp ....

crisp ....

smooth ....

rough ....

bumpy ....

What is the tickliest thing that you can find?

Draw a picture of it here

Ask a friend to hold his
hands behind his back, test
his hand with one of your
'feely' things and see if he
can guess what you are testing him with.

Find a long piece of string and spread it out along the grass or the pavement. Find as many different textured natural things as you can (remember not to pick whole plants!) and space them out along the string.

Here is a trail you might like to try:

START HERE

twig

feathers

blades of grass

dandelion

privet leaf

moss

holly

THE END

Blindfold a friend and ask her to walk along your trail with her hands and guess what each thing is! Then take the blindfold off and take her back along the trail to see if she guessed right!

Ask your friend to design a trail for you.

Hug a
tree!

Find a place where there are some trees (they can be big
or small.)

How many trees can you see? ....

What do they have in common?

....

....

In what ways are they different?

....

....

Choose one tree that you think looks interesting. With
your eyes closed give it a hug. What does it feel like?

Sniff it! What does it smell of?
Feel the bark, and stretch your arms up. Can you reach
any branches or leaves?

Sit down next to it and feel around the bottom of the
trunk. Are there any roots?

Ask a friend to close his eyes and lead him to your tree.

Without opening his eyes ask him to make friends with the tree and find out as much about it as he can.

Lead him away from the tree (still with eyes closed!). Turn him around three times, then ask him to open his eyes and try and find the same tree again!

Now it's your turn to make friends with a tree.

What do you notice about it?

....

....

....

....

Can you find the same tree again?

Tree pictures!

Which tree do these leaves belong to?

1.
These trees
can live for
400 years!

2.
This is used
as a
Christmas
decoration!

....

3.
The wood
from this
tree is very
hard. Good
for making
furniture!

4.
You can
play
conkers
with the
fruit of this
tree.

....

5.
The seeds
of this tree
have wings
to help
them float
away!

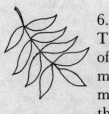

6.
The handle
of a spade
might be
made from
this tree!

....

How many different leaves can you find?

Make a leaf print by covering the top side of a leaf with paint (use a sponge or cottonwool). Press the leaf face down on a plain piece of paper, then lift it off to see the picture you have made!

You can make your prints any colour you like, to make a picture. Or you could try matching the colour of the leaf exactly.

Put a leaf between two sheets of soft paper (tissue, or kitchen roll will do), weight them down with some heavy books. When the leaf is dry, after about two weeks, stick it into a book and write its name beside it. You could make your own tree book to help you recognise trees.

Wild cherry

Have a look underneath a leaf. How is it different from the top? ....

Another way of recognising a tree is by its bark.

With some plain or greaseproof paper and a dark wax crayon, you can take your own picture of tree bark by making a bark rubbing.

Hold the paper against the bark, or stick it on with sticky tape,

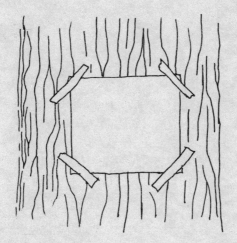

rub over the paper with the crayon and watch the pattern of the bark appear.

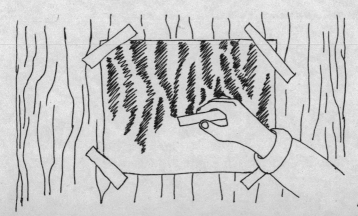

Can you spot how the leaves change colour in the autumn as they begin to die?

Use this page to make your own tree pictures with prints, drawings and bark rubbings. . . .

Self seeders!

Each tree has its own fruit or seed which plants itself (with help from animals or wind!).

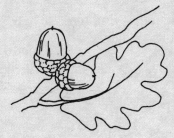

Acorns come from oak trees. Some animals like to eat acorns, but they also help to plant oak trees because they store their food in holes ready to eat in the winter and then sometimes forget where they have put it!

Can you think of any animals that do this?

Try planting an acorn in the neck of a bottle full of water. Watch it and its roots grow!

Conkers are the fruit of the horse chestnut tree. They plant themselves when they fall off.

Beechnuts are hidden inside a prickly husk. Squirrels and pigeons love eating them!

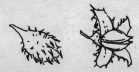

We can eat the sweet chestnut (usually roasted first). It's too cold in Britain for the chestnuts to grow very big. Most of the ones we eat come from abroad.

Pine cones are like big seed pods. The wind shakes the seeds they contain to the ground.

Sycamore seeds have wings so they can float away on the wind. Sometimes they twist like helicopter blades!

Ash and lime seeds are planted on the wind too – so new trees are found growing in all sorts of places.

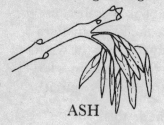

ASH

LIME

How many tree seeds can you collect in the autumn! ....

Draw the seeds you find here.

Do you know which trees they come from?

Try throwing some of the seeds into the air and see which one the wind carries the furthest.

Dead plants!

Have you ever blown a dandelion clock to see what time it is? Did you know that by doing that you have planted many more dandelions?

Each dandelion seed is like a small parachute carried on the wind.

Dandelion seeds   **DANDELION**

When a flower dies, it leaves behind it a seed pod. When the pod blows in the wind seeds are planted ready for a new plant to grow the following year!

Can you spot seed pods from these flowers?

POPPIES   **NASTURTIUMS**

LUPINS

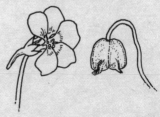

Try collecting some weeds — plant them in earth in a yoghurt pot, and wait to see what grows!

Next time you are out, look around you and see if you can spot any flowers growing in unusual places – in walls or on top of buildings. How do you think they were planted there?

You can also plant things indoors. . . .

Next time you eat an orange save a pip and plant it in a pot. Keep it in a dark place until the shoots begin to grow. Then bring it out into the light and water it regularly.

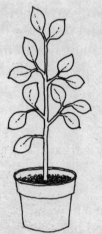

ORANGE PLANT

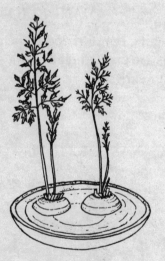

Save some carrot tops and stand them in a saucer of water. Watch the green shoots grow!

CARROT TOPS

Experiment with other pips, beans or vegetable tops and grow your own indoor garden!

Birds of prey!

Birds of prey have hooked beaks and strong claws for catching their prey. They eat animals, snakes, fish, insects and other birds. You are most likely to spot them when they are in flight.

Can you spot . . .

A Buzzard?

Broad wings

Broad tail

Buzzards can be spotted all over Britain. They have broad wings and broad tails and very good eyesight! When hunting they fly round and round in wide slow circles.

A Kestrel?

A kestrel belongs to the falcon family. It can be spotted hovering in the air, with its fan-shaped tail spread out, waiting to swoop down on its prey and carry it off.

Long pointed wings   Long tail

You may spot a kestrel hovering near a motorway or a busy road.

All hawks have short rounded wings and long tails.

A sparrowhawk?

The sparrowhawk often hunts in the hedgerow, mounting surprise attacks on small birds. It can plunge out of the sky with folded wings.

A golden eagle?

Golden eagles are very rare! They have very broad wings – as wide as two metres from tip to tip, and can swoop on their prey at up to 90 miles per hour. They are usually found in the Highlands of Scotland.

Wide tail

Very wide wings

An owl?

Most owls hunt at night, but if you spot an owl hunting in daylight, then it is probably a short-eared owl. Its 'ears' are really small tufts of feathers!

Broad head   Short tail

What other birds of prey can you spot? ....

....

48

On the trail!

Be a detective on the trail! Can you spot where an animal lives? Or where it has been?

Some clues to look for:

Droppings	Footprints
Food remains	Broken twigs or undergrowth
Hairs	Scratches on bark

All good detectives keep a notebook!

Make a note of places where you spot hairs. What do you think they belong to?

Hairs can be a good clue to where an animal lives – animals often stop to scratch or groom themselves by the entrance to their home.

Food remains are strong evidence that an animal lives nearby. If you think you know where an animal lives, put some food near its home. Hide and see if it is tempted to come out.

What can you spot? ....

....

If you spot some tracks or droppings you could draw them carefully, and identify them later.

You could take some evidence home with you!

Make a plaster cast of footprints:

Bend a strip of strong card into a circle and join the ends together.

Place this around the track and push it into the ground.

Make a thick, creamy plaster of Paris mixture with water.

Pour the plaster of Paris into the ring and leave it to set.

Lift up the mould, remove the ring and paint the print.

See how many different prints you can collect.

Feeding clues! If you find food remains, you might be able to tell who has been eating it.

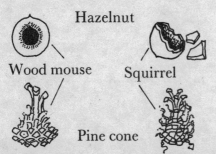

Hazelnut

Wood mouse

Squirrel

Pine cone

If you find something nibbled round the edges, it is evidence that a house mouse has been eating.

If you want to spot an animal, then try and make sure it doesn't spot you first!

Remember:
Wear dull clothes.
Hide behind or amongst bushes.
Be as quiet as possible.

Animals often have a keen sense of smell and may be better detectives than you are. If you spot an animal move round until the wind is blowing in your face – it will be less likely to pick up your scent.

Sit above the ground on a branch – the wind will carry your scent over the animal's head.

: Be careful when climbing trees – if you fall off you might hurt yourself and you will certainly frighten any wildlife away!

If you spot something and there is nowhere to hide, crawl nearer on your stomach. Freeze if the animal looks up.

Good Luck!

Spotting
in the dark!

Can you see in the dark? If not a torch may help!
Animals are disturbed by bright light, so cover the face of
your torch with red cellophane or sweet papers.

Can you spot . . .

You might as easily spot a
fox in the town as in the
country. They hunt or
scavenge in dustbins under
cover of night.

A fox?

Owls hunt at night, when
small animals are active.
You may hear them
hooting, screeching or
flapping their wings before
you see them.

An owl?

Badgers play, as well as hunt, at night! In the dark the white stripes on their faces show up like a strange skull to frighten away their enemies.

A Badger?

or
**SPOT
THE
DIFFERENCE**

A stoat?   A weasel?

Stoats and weasels look very alike. Stoats are larger than weasels and have a longer tail with a black tip at its end. They hunt by sound and smell rather than sight. Keep very still if you spot one.

Otters are very difficult to spot. They live by rivers and the sea, and often wander long distances at night, while hunting.

An otter?

What have you spotted at night? ....

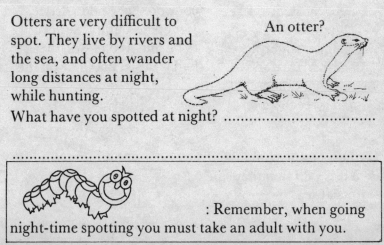

: Remember, when going night-time spotting you must take an adult with you.

Be a
weather reporter

Have you heard the saying 'red sky at night shepherd's delight, red sky in the morning shepherd's warning?'

Do you think it's true? Next time you see a red sky, try predicting the weather and see if you're right.

Have you ever noticed a group of cows lying down under the trees on a fine day? Some people say this is a sign that it is going to rain. What do you think?

You could try predicting the weather by putting a pine cone on the window-ledge. If it opens out it is supposed to be fine. If it closes, then bad weather could be on the way!

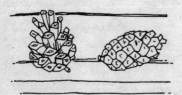

If you spot a seagull inland, then it is said that there are storms at sea.

54

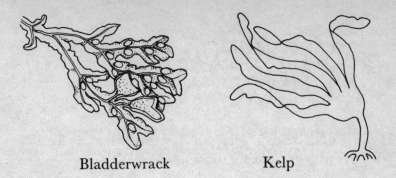

Bladderwrack   Kelp

If you go to the seaside, try to bring some seaweed home.
(Bladderwrack or Kelp would be best). Dry it out
indoors, then hang a bunch outside in a place where it
can't be rained on. If it goes floppy then it is said that the
weather will turn damp. If it stays crisp, then it should
stay fine!

Make a weather chart and see if you can predict the
weather.

METHOD	WHAT HAPPENS	WEATHER – Good	WEATHER – Bad
e.g. Pine cones	open	✓	

Small
pets!

If you would like to look after a very small creature for a few days why not look for some woodlice?

You will easily spot them outdoors under stones, bricks or damp wood.

An old shoe box with a lid makes a comfortable home. Woodlice like to live in damp, dark places, but they also need air so punch a few holes in the lid, and then sprinkle the inside of the box with water to keep it damp.

Rotting wood and damp leaves are the favourite food of the woodlouse so put a food store inside the box as well.

When you have found your woodlice, lift three or four of them gently with a piece of paper and put them into their new home.

Keep the box in a cool place.

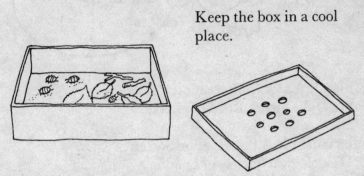

If you would like to have a closer look, take a woodlouse out onto the palm of your hand.

How many legs can you count? (A magnifying glass might come in useful.) ....

Can you spot the breathing gills at the ends of its front six legs? ....

Can you spot its feelers? ....

or its eyes? ....

Turn it over. . . . Can you find its mouth? ....

Turn the woodlouse onto its back and watch it turn itself over.

Can you spot anything else about the woodlice?

Remember to keep the box damp and supplied with food, then after four or five days put the woodlice back where you found them.

Useful addresses

British Trust for Conservation Volunteers,
10–14 Duke Street, Reading, Berks.

Fauna and Flora Preservation Society,
C/O Zoological Society of London,
Regents Park, London NW1 4RY.

The Nature Conservancy Council,
Northminster House, Peterborough PE1 1UA .

People's Dispensary for Sick Animals,
Busy Bees Club, P.D.S.A. House,
South Street, Dorking, Surrey.

R.S.P.C.A. Junior Membership,
Causeway, Horsham, Sussex RH12 1HG.

Watch Trust for Environmental Education Ltd.,
22 The Green, Nettleham, Lincoln LN2 2NR.

Young Ornithologists Club,
R.S.P.B., The Lodge, Sandy, Beds.